MAKING SENSE OF BEHAVIOUR

DEVELOPING SELF-ESTEEM THROUGH POSITIVE ENTRAPMENT FOR PUPILS FACING EMOTIONAL AND BEHAVIOURAL DIFFICULTIES

by

Rob Long

A NASEN PUBLICATION

Published in 1999

ISBN 1 901485 07 2

Published by NASEN.
NASEN is a company limited by guarantee, registered in England and Wales. Company No. 2674379.
NASEN is a registered charity. Charity No. 1007023.

Further copies of this book and details of NASEN's many other publications may be obtained from the Publications Department at its registered office: NASEN House, 4/5 Amber Business Village, Amber Close, Amington, Tamworth, Staffs. B77 4RP.
Tel: 01827 311500; Fax: 01827 313005
Email: welcome@nasen.org.uk; Website: www.nasen.org.uk

Cover design by Raphael Creative Design.
Typeset in Times by J. C. Typesetting and printed in the United Kingdom by Stowes (Stoke-on-Trent).

Contents

Preface   4

Introduction   5

What is positive entrapment?   5

Understanding emotions   7

Strategies   10

Solution Focussed Interview Planner   10

Self-Esteem   11

Positive Thinking   14

Activities   17

Special Time   18

Positive Entrapment Record   21

Preface

Developing Self-esteem through Positive Entrapment for Pupils facing Emotional and Behavioural Difficulties is one of eight booklets in the series *Making Sense of Behaviour* by Rob Long. The others are *Understanding and Supporting Depressed Children and Young People; Exercising Self-control; Friendships; Not Me, Miss! The Truth about Children who Lie; Challenging Confrontation: Information and Techniques for School Staff; Supporting Pupils with Emotional and Behavioural Difficulties through Consistency;* and *Learning to Wave: Some Everyday Guidelines for Stress Management.*

The first five titles give practical ideas and information for teachers to use with children with worrying behaviours in their classes. These are written to help teachers both understand and change some of the difficulties that children might experience (depression, lack of self-control, low self-esteem, friendship problems and lying).

Challenging Confrontation gives information and techniques for teachers to use when dealing with argumentative, angry and difficult pupils. *Supporting Pupils with Emotional and Behavioural Difficulties through Consistency* advocates a whole-school approach for low-level misbehaviours whilst *Learning to Wave* is written for teachers themselves. It contains advice about coping with the stress which might arise from dealing with children with behavioural problems.

Each book stands alone but when read as a set the behavioural issues and their solutions overlap and this emphasises the need for positive and consistent strategies to be put into place throughout the school.

Acknowledgements
The author and publishers wish to express their grateful thanks to Lorna Johnston, Agnes Donnelly and Dorothy Smith for their helpful suggestions and comments.

Developing Self-esteem through Positive Entrapment for pupils facing emotional and behavioural difficulties

Introduction

The majority of children who are described as having emotional and behavioural difficulties are not happy children. For many it is their emotional difficulties that cause their negative behaviour. If they have been rejected, hurt or abused, have faced loss or have very specific medical difficulties, then their reactions are understandable. They are troubled children.

There are children who have learned to behave the way they do. Perhaps they have come to believe that aggression does pay: that being disruptive in class can help them avoid difficult work; or perhaps that being troublesome does get them an increase in attention, albeit angry attention. Now while we as adults may see this attention as being negative, if children crave attention then any sort of attention will do.

This booklet is aimed at providing strategies to raise the self-esteem of pupils who face emotional and behavioural difficulties. While many of the ideas have relevance to children of all ages and abilities it is primarily for children between 8 and 14 years. It will be most effective with those children who are able to achieve a degree of insight and understanding into their thoughts, feelings and actions.

What is positive entrapment?

Positive Entrapment is a range of techniques that support a child's emotional well-being. It is based on the assumption that children with emotional and behavioural difficulties cannot possibly be obtaining enough positive input because the nature of their difficulty prevents this. In other words their behaviour is trapped in always leading to negative feedback and outcomes from both adults and peers. A few examples will show this clearly.

1. Tom is 8 years old and is facing a range of difficulties at home. He lives with his terminally ill stepfather and mother, and sees his alcoholic father from time to time. In school he is extremely volatile, running around erratically during playtimes, frequently hitting other children.

In class his attention-seeking behaviour results in frequent reprimands. With friends he tends to be physically "all over them", hugging and kissing them. This results in friends withdrawing from him which in turn makes Tom frustrated and aggressive.

2. Claire is 14 years old and finds much of her work difficult. In class she is quick-tempered and overtly rude to the support assistants who work with her. Her bad language has resulted in several fixed-term exclusions but Claire sees the problems she has experienced in school as mainly the fault of the adults. If they left her alone there would be no problem.

These examples show how children develop ways of coping with difficult circumstances. It is not unusual for them to fall into what is known as a "negative emotional feedback cycle". This means that the very behaviour we would most wish to change becomes stronger and harder to break. For example, the child who misbehaves to obtain attention, may find adults being angry with them at first, but subsequently becoming "cold" and less friendly towards them. This fuels the child's anger and frustration leading to more misbehaviour. See the diagram below.

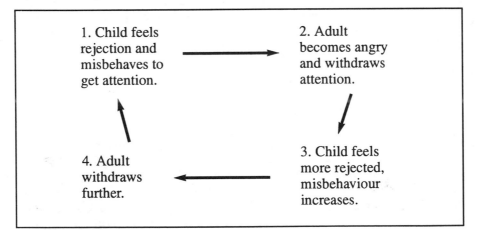

Negative Emotional Feedback Cycle

Adults and schools get drawn into this cycle and often seek more effective sanctions to control the child's behaviour. But if sanctions alone were the solution then there would not be a problem. Sanctions clearly do have the desired effect on most children. Children are motivated to want adult approval, not disapproval. Therefore, when they find the boundaries that control their behaviour, sanctions keep them away from them. Here we are talking about children who go up to the boundaries daily, if not hourly. "How many times must I tell you to put your hand up when you need help?" The answer is, "you name it" - and then add some. The negative feedback such children receive is essential for their negative emotional needs. It is a self-perpetuating vicious circle.

Understanding emotions

Emotions make up the internal driving force that shapes our experiences and motivates us to behave in certain ways. They give our lives colour and enhance our experiences. Most of the time children experience positive emotions, those associated with being loved, belonging and trusting. These in turn allow other positive emotions to emerge: curiosity, sharing and mastery. We can view a child's emotional development as being like a building. The foundations must be secure for the first floor to stand soundly. If the foundations are weak then this will affect later development. Similarly if a child, for whatever reason, does not experience a loving and trusting relationship during infancy then the lack of trust will echo through and affect later development. Such children will have an echo of not trusting others throughout their lives, unless it is positively addressed.

We all have emotional issues like this. Even if we were brought up in the "perfect family", there will be issues that provide the emotional grist to the mill that shapes our personality. (People who have no emotional challenges, worries or issues are probably more in need of help than the rest of us, who know we are slightly neurotic.)

Negative emotions give shape and meaning to the positive ones. It is impossible to conceive of a situation where we lose a loved one but feel no sadness. Such emotions as anger, sadness and despair are as essential for us as joy and happiness. (It is a sign of increasing emotional maturity when children recognise that an event can give rise to two, possibly conflicting, emotions.)

BUT because such emotions exist they will always look for ways of controlling and dominating us. They are not content to just sit around

7

until genuinely needed, they will look for opportunities to take the limelight. Our language and behaviour become ideal ways in which they seek to gain expression. We can see these "emotional gremlins" at work through our thoughts and behaviour. They can result in Negative Entrapment.

Examples of negative entrapment:

- I don't believe I'm likeable, so to test you as a friend I will be nasty to the point where you reject me, which confirms my hunch that I am unlikeable.
- I am so useless at everything that it is a waste of time trying to succeed, which just highlights how inadequate I really am.
- Because I am not as good as the other children, you will only notice me when I am naughty, which shows how naughty I am.
- I am so angry at not being liked, that I try too hard to get you to like me, and it makes me angry if you reject me.
- I feel so lonely and scared of being left on my own that I firmly attach myself to new people to the point that they reject me, leaving me on my own, which is what I am scared of.

Remember children will not necessarily be able to give an account of why they do what they do. We are inferring from their behaviour a script that can help us to understand what is going on for the child. We always assume that reasons are within a child's reach, and while this can be so, it is not always the case. (This will be especially true for children with autism.) Most of our memories are laid down using language. We can therefore recall through language what happened to us, especially those memories that have emotional significance to us. But if the emotional experience happened before we had language then the emotional memory will still be part of us, and affect us, but we will be unable to recall it through language because it is not encoded in language. (A similar example is when certain smells bring back memories we previously had no recollection of.) Emotional memories exist and influence us even though we cannot recall them through language, and they can be positive as well as negative. A child who experienced strong emotions of fear during infancy may show signs of nervousness and apprehension in new situations. No matter how much we ask them "Why?", they will be unable to explain why, though they may "make up" some plausible reasons. (There are of course other reasons why a child might be nervous in new situations.) We see the

8

positive influence of past emotional experiences in the confident and trusting way most children approach new situations. Positive Entrapment can help children who have negative emotional memories.

Positive Entrapment
Positive Entrapment is more than just a way of rewarding appropriate behaviour. Children who respond to such approaches are not trapped in emotional negativity. Positive Entrapment is for those who seem not to respond to our usual common sense approaches, or, if they do, any improvements are short-lived. An analogy would be that most people with a cold respond well to paracetamol, hot drinks and TLC. But there are times when antibiotics are needed. Positive Entrapment is the antibiotic for those most difficult to reach children whose troubled and/or troublesome behaviours are resistant to all our efforts.

Positive Entrapment:
- increases self-esteem
- challenges negative thinking
- uses actions to promote success
- promotes positive relationships
- breaks negative cycles
- sees personal success as a right not a possibility

It is not:
- a quick fix
- just about rewards
- only about behaviour

The following pages describe techniques from the key areas presented below. To design an all-encompassing Positive Entrapment Programme it is recommended that techniques from as many of the areas as possible are included. The effects of such a programme will be seen over weeks and months rather than days. In situations where little or no change is seen, then your efforts should be maintained. Our actions should not always be determined by immediate outcomes. If you believe that what you are doing is the right thing then keep doing it. (However, we must take care not to blindly persist with strategies which are showing no signs of success. We need to be clear as to what will be small signs of improvement. Children can suffer when adults blindly persist with inappropriate strategies.)

9

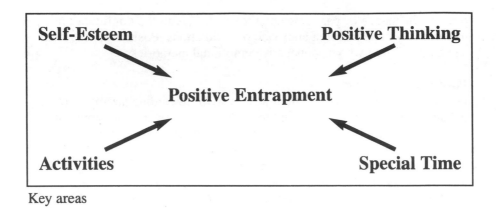

Key areas

Strategies   Using WFGs Qs

Solution-Focused Interview Planner

Before we begin to consider the specific strategies available to achieve Positive Entrapment we need an appropriate interview framework, one that shifts the emphasis from the negative to the positive. Such an approach comes from "Solution-Focused Brief Therapy". While this was originally used in Family Therapy it is ideally suited to us. It can be summed up as "bring me the solution not the problem". Below is an interview schedule based on this approach. The focus is not on the problem but on the solution and signs of improvement. Instead of expecting total improvement this approach asks pupils to notice the slightest signs of improvement. Pupils are asked to indicate how they will know when situations are improving, the smallest sign, and then to go and make them happen. The language naturally needs to be adapted for children - but it can clarify our own thoughts, decisions and actions.

Signs of improvement
Since you agreed to try to improve your behaviour have you noticed any signs that things are better? Are you better in any lessons? Are some of your playtimes better? Has anyone said "well done"?

Finding the exceptions
You know that there are times when you work really well and play with your friends. When is it like that? Why do you think you are so good at such times? What's going on that is helping you?

10

Scaling concerns

On a scale of 1-10 with 0 being the absolute worst and 10 how you want things to be, where are you today? What are you doing that puts you at 3 and not 0? (Children rarely see themselves as being at 0.) What is it that you need to be doing more of to move them up to say a 4 or a 5?)

Goal setting

When it is difficult for the child to decide their goal the Miracle Question can help. Say you go home, you go to bed tonight, you're asleep and a miracle happens and the difficulty we are working on is resolved. Since you are asleep you won't know about the miracle. When you come to school tomorrow how will you know things are better? What will you be doing differently? If this is beyond the pupil's understanding focus on a specific short-term goal with agreed positive incentives for success.

Feedback and tasks

Feed back to the child the skills and qualities you notice about them. Clearly explain what you think they are doing that is helping to improve matters. Set NOTICING TASKS, "try to notice all those times when things are going on the right track" and DOING TASKS, when you feel confident that they can succeed, "I want you to practise this throughout the week..."

Follow-up

Always stress what the child is doing differently that is part of the solution and moving things on. "So what do you notice that tells you that things are beginning to get better?"

Self-Esteem

Children with emotional and behavioural difficulties receive far less positive feedback from all of the key people in their lives. They will receive little positive feedback about their behaviour in class and school. Often their peers find their volatility and unpredictability difficult to manage and will often withdraw from them. It is not unusual to find such children at secondary school mixing mainly with each other, which can generate as many problems as it solves as they can be "their own worst enemy". With their school work suffering as well, their academic success is low. Their parents may also tire of having to come into school on account of their problem behaviour. Parents who have themselves a poor memory of their own schooling can hardly be expected to lift their children's spirits when theirs are low. The following techniques have been proven to be essential for healthy mental health. A balanced diet will ensure that a child is receiving the correct input to challenge negative feelings and instil positive ones.

Exercise
Exercise releases adrenalin which makes us naturally feel more positive. It can be anything from walking, swimming or group sports. The important thing is to do some form of activity at least three times a week and for some 20-30 minutes at a time.

Humour
Laughing is not only a form of exercise as it can also release tensions and worries. Finding something each day that makes us smile is a healthy activity anyway.

Good news
Many children find it incredibly difficult to recall some good news from their week. Set this as a task. Give them a list of examples to choose from that will help them to see the positive events in their lives and not just the negative ones.

Target setting
Encourage children to set agreed targets, that are naturally achievable and desirable. A built-in reward can be agreed. When targets are achieved our confidence is boosted. Make them short in time in order that they will achieve.

Relaxation
While children vary as to how they like to relax, encourage your children to have quiet times. Do they watch TV, take their dog for a walk, or play a gentle game? We all need "nothing time" to unwind from the day and children are no different.

Diary keeping
Help the child to keep a diary noting especially those times they do things they enjoy. Encourage them to see how often they do such activities and try to increase them.

Positive linking

Teach the child to remember a special place where they were really happy. What were they doing? What were they wearing? What could they see and smell? With practice they will be able to elicit this memory, and the positive feelings associated with it when they wish to. It can help them overcome negative feelings.

MY DAILY ACTIVITY PLAN
Each day I will:

Exercise through:

....

....

....

....

Relax through:

....

....

....

....

The target I am working towards:

....

....

....

At the end of each day I will keep a diary of what I have enjoyed, what made me laugh and what I plan to do tomorrow.

My next special treat for keeping to my plan is that I will:

....on................................

Positive Thinking

It is understandable that many children, especially those experiencing emotional and behavioural difficulties, develop a negative view of themselves. These tend to be reinforced through being used regularly, as well as young people selectively choosing information which confirms the negative view of themselves. The Pupil Record Form displayed on page 16 is an example of a record that children of any age can be either helped or encouraged to fill in as a record of their positive attributes.

Skill recognition
Over a period of time an adult repetitively focuses in on specific competencies that the child has. "I liked the way you completed that picture yesterday, you have a good eye for colours." At the same time children are asked to give examples of skills they have acquired. This can be a very difficult exercise for many and the adult should be prepared to give examples or remind them of something they had observed the children doing.

Evocative words
Words can and do encourage feelings that correspond to them. For example words like, "control", "power", have a positive impact, while "sad", "weak", etc pull the opposite way. It is good for children to have a range of special words. These will need to be used and practised frequently. Provide a range of words for them to choose from. Some examples are:

> helpful   caring   interested   sensitive   sharing
> funny   kind   dependable   honest   loyal   open
> creative   purposeful   happy   enthusiastic
> friendly   strong   independent

This may also be the time to teach some children how to describe their feelings.

Coping thoughts
To challenge the existing negative ones such as, "I'm no good at this", or "I can't cope with this", we need to develop a range of well-rehearsed ones that instil a sense of purpose and commitment. While teachers can design their own with the child, the following examples should be included.

1. Convey past success, "I've managed this before and it was OK."
2. Reflect a small step, "Little by little I am improving."
3. Minimalise outcomes, "Even if the worst happens I know I will be alright."

Positive thoughts

Have the child complete a range of positive sentences and then set them the task of learning two or three off by heart. Make testing fun. Examples:

One thing I always do well is ....

My friends like me because...

A happy memory was when I...

Something I've improved in lately is...

One thing I like about me is ....

I can always be depended on to...

People like it when I...

I know I can ....

One of my best qualities is ....

These are to be learned and practised daily.

Thought stopping

Teach the child that if they ever find themselves thinking negative thoughts then to imagine that they can see a big bright light in their heads saying STOP. Then it changes to THINK. They then have to quickly say under their breath five positive thoughts about themselves.

MY SUCCESS RECORD

Name:...

Skills I have learned:

....
....
....
....
....
....

Skills I am learning:

....
....
....
....
....
....
....

Positive thoughts:

1. ....
2. ....
3. ....
4. ....
5. ....

My key words:

....

Activities

There are many activities that can be used that serve several purposes at the same time. Most will be beneficial to all but there will be some that are especially appropriate to children with certain needs. For example, children who have a strong desire to be in control will benefit from structured responsibilities, while less confidant children will have their esteem boosted when they help others. With some children the very lack of determination is part of their difficulty. They can often have the right solution but because they lack the will power to continue they fail. The strategies below will address all these issues.

Helping

There are several key components to this strategy which make it a very useful approach. The helper will use conversation skills and by listening will have the experience of being trusted and depended upon. Firstly let's say a child has a difficulty, this is the focus child. The focus child offers to help another child and the offer is accepted. Between them they design a plan to solve the problem and then implement the plan. Let's say that perhaps with some adult input, the problem gets solved.

The helper feels of value and the child who has been helped feels gratitude for the assistance. Ideally there is an exchange of thanks and goodwill between the two.

Note the positive skills and experiences that are involved.

> Problem solving and decision making skills
> Delayed gratification
> Co-operation
> Coping with frustration when solutions fail
> Learning through exploration and discovery
> Pleasure when solutions work

Also for those who have experienced rejection it is the best antidote to the fear of loneliness. They will experience approval and gratitude for their efforts and not rejection and hostility. So whenever a child is engaged in a helping task you should sit back and experience a warm glow because you have provided, in one activity, a whole range of experiences that are psychologically good for that child's mental health. (In the real world preparation and planning will help ensure maximum effectiveness.)

Responsibilities

Being given genuine responsibilities to do over a period of time can carry with it a number of benefits. Children experience being trusted and it can help them develop a routine. Classroom jobs may seem mundane but they have a part to play. Some examples include putting today's date on the board, register monitor, plant watering etc.

Carrying out requests

It is not uncommon for some children with behavioural difficulties to be defiant when asked by adults to carry our certain tasks. Whatever they are asked to do they reply with "no". Instead of avoiding asking them to help, it is better to make a point of involving them. On a daily basis make a point of asking them to do very small tasks. "Could you just pass me that ruler?" This is to get them used to complying to reasonable requests. Once a week they could become Class Support Worker, a position that carries with it the expectation that they will carry out a range of helping activities.

Will power

Will power can be developed and strengthened through carrying out certain activities. They can seem questionable to the uninitiated but they will help. If children lack the ability to complete tasks then set them "heroic acts of trivia", for example having to sharpen all pencils and sort them into colours. Or, providing it is safe, set a child the challenge of completing so many laps of the circuit. The point is that some children rarely complete any tasks and therefore never have that satisfied experience of "a job well done". Other examples could be finishing a game of chess or playing with someone they usually don't get on with.

Special Time

The children we are most concerned with here are the ones that many adults find difficult to include. Their behaviour can make them the least likeable. Their language can be offensive and those who have been sexually abused can relate to us in ways that make us both apprehensive and unsure of what to do. These are the children with whom we constantly have to go the "extra mile". But behaviour that is learned can be unlearned, and behind every challenging behaviour is a child who is unconditionally likeable. But how do we get to them? Research has shown that children who face emotional and behavioural difficulties are less likely to be

18

excluded if they experience genuine care and respect from one adult. These adults as "charismatic heroes" seem to provide the child with the courage, respect and determination which are required for coping more successfully with the challenges they face in school.

The suggestions below are more appropriate for a classroom assistant than a class teacher. This is because it could be difficult for a class teacher to resume the role of teacher after they have become involved in a close 1:1 relationship with a vulnerable child. It might also be difficult for some children to cope with the switch. The "befriender role" is best filled by an adult or assistant rather than the teacher.

Problem free time
Any time spent 1:1 with a child is invaluable, but because the talk is so often problem-orientated, problem free time is invaluable. This involves the focus being on what the focus child enjoys doing, hobbies and the like. The adult's aim is to learn about the child's qualities and skills. Being given an adult's undivided attention on matters in which the child is an expert themselves, will help develop a relationship. The adult's attitude should be one of "you teach me about who you are." At such times we are listening with our eyes, ears and heart. Make a point of giving "I" messages, "I like it when you …" Make sure that children know that you value their efforts as much as their achievements. Turn the letters of their name into a positive list of qualities and skills.

Self-disclosure
All children enjoy it when adults reveal personal information. This is going behind the role of being a teacher and pupil to the real person. Revealing such matters as your favourite meal, music, TV soap etc will help build a relationship. It can of course be a game where similarities and differences are looked for and valued equally.

Expectations and belief
Children who have experienced little success will have low expectations and negative beliefs about themselves. They will in all probability believe that they can make little difference. Communicate your positive expectations to them. Let them know that while there may be an occasional blip, you do not doubt that they are going to succeed. You can see the challenges and obstacles they face and have faith in them. Short notes etc whenever you see them rise to the challenge will be kept and treasured by the child. "I

was so impressed yesterday when you offered to share the computer with John. Well done." "It makes me feel so proud when I see how hard you are trying to listening fully in class. Keep it up."

Humour

Jokes can be a dangerous area. However, jokes can show how close a relationship is. There needs to be a clear and determined insistence, though, that jokes are appropriate and not made at the expense of any groups. Through finding the same things funny we are showing that we share the same reality.

The ideas presented in this booklet are intended to compliment the many everyday activities that all teachers and support staff use to develop and maintain children's sense of confidence. It will be most helpful for those few children who seem resistant to all our efforts. Positive entrapment is a way of ensuring that such a child is receiving their "mental health" vitamins on a regular and systematic basis. To this end the record form (which follows) can be usefully completed to record the definite actions that have been taken to support children who lack confidence.

Positive Entrapment Record

For: ....

Completed by: ....

Date: ....

SPECIAL TIME
achieved through

1. ....

2. ....

3. ....

4. ....

ACTIVITIES
achieved through

1. ....

2. ....

3. ....

4. ....

POSITIVE THINKING
achieved through

1. ....
   ....

2. ....
   ....

3. ....
   ....

4. ....

SELF-ESTEEM
achieved through

1. ....
   ....

2. ....
   ....

3. ....
   ....

4. ....

Review by Date: ....

References

Deiro, A. (1996) *Teaching With Heart*, Corwin Press, Inc.: California.

Strayhorn, J. M. (1988) *The Competent Child*, The Guilford Press: New York.